This book belongs to

_______________________________

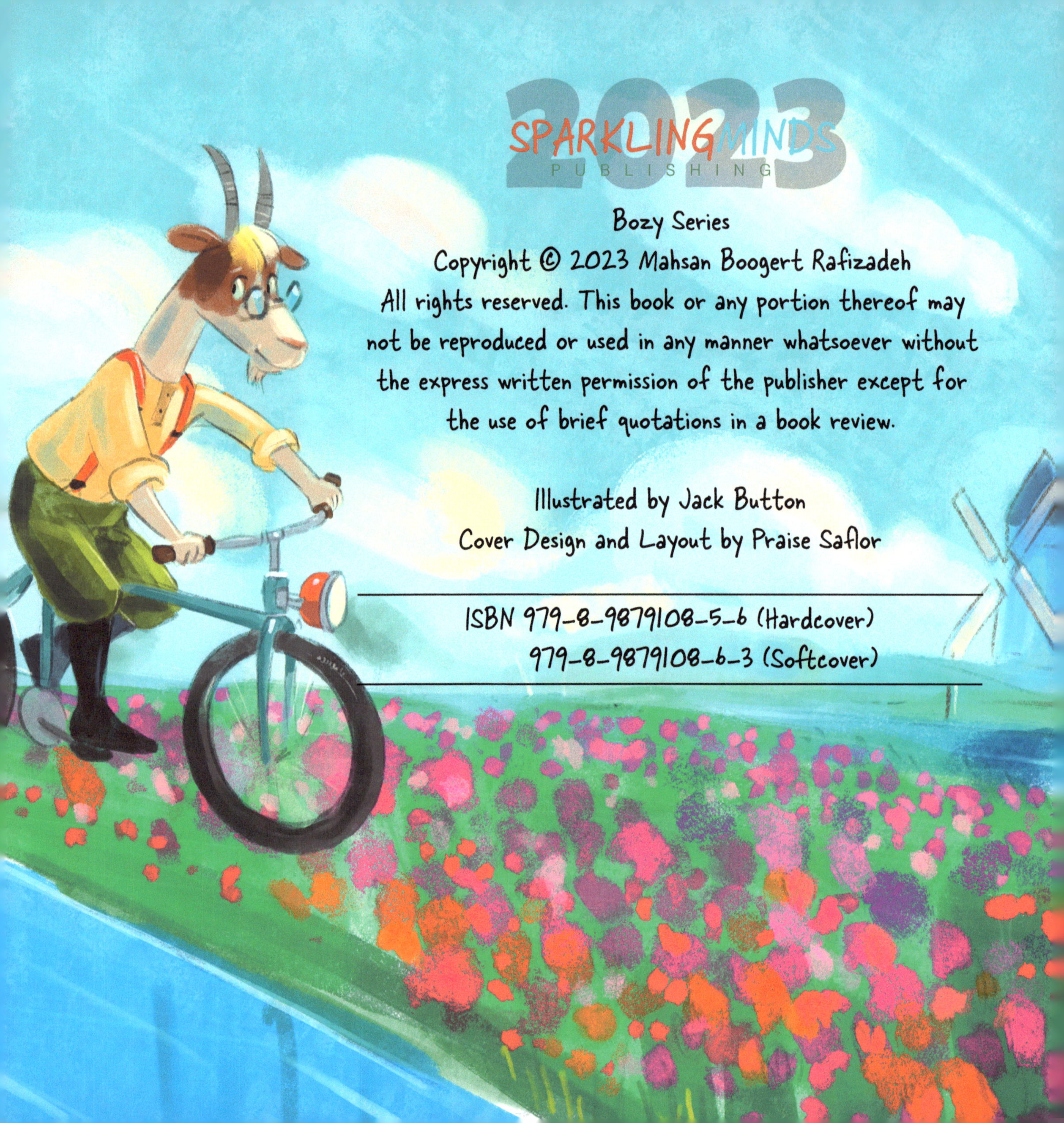




Illustrated by Jack Button
Cover Design and Layout by Praise Saflor

ISBN 979-8-9879108-5-6 (Hardcover)
979-8-9879108-6-3 (Softcover)

Welcome to the
Kinderdijk
By Mahsan Boogert
Art by Jack Button

Hi Friends! This is Bozy the goat!

Have you ever seen a real windmill? They're super tall, and have long, twirling arms that go 'round and 'round when the wind swishes by. It looks like they're having the happiest dance-off ever.

I know a magical village named Kinderdijk. It's in a country called the Netherlands—a dreamy place filled with lots of windmills. The people in the Netherlands are called Dutch. If you're up for an adventure, let's go visit Kinderdijk. You will be amazed at the most fantastic windmills you've ever seen!

Here we are at Kinderdijk!

Let's jump on our bikes and go on
a fun-filled adventure to discover
all the amazing things in this village.

Wow, check this out! See that giant spinning thing? It's one of the windmills, and it's a superhero for this village. The land here is lower than the water, so when it rains, it's like a giant puddle party. But these handsome windmills, with their tall towers and spinning blades, swoop in and keep the land—and our toesies—nice and dry!

Let's go inside one of the windmills.

It feels like we're going on an adventure into
a secret hideout! Are you scared? Don't be!
We can climb up the stairs and watch the big blades
spinning around. And guess what? We might even
get to meet the miller and his family.

Welcome to the first floor. It's a living room, kitchen, and bedroom all in one. It's SO cute and cozy! And check out the box-bed! Have you ever seen one in a kitchen! It's incredibly adorable and keeps you cozy and warm when winter comes!

Now, are you wondering what you can cook
in such a tiny kitchen?

Dutch people eat really tasty and healthy foods.
Let's take a look at some of them.

One of their favorite meals is Hutspot. It's made with mashed potatoes, onions, and carrots. It tastes even better if you eat it with smoked sausage. Yum!

Also, Dutch people eat special donuts called Oliebollen. They are super tasty, and the people love to eat them when they celebrate the New Year!

Let's take a little trip upstairs, shall we?

Welcome to the second floor! Here you'll see more beds. This is where the miller's children sleep, and also where they play when it's too cold to go outside.

Did you know that millers have furry and feathered helpers like cows, sheep, and chickens? They're all part of a big, happy family, working together to make the village lively and joyful!

And guess what? With the milk from their cows, the people make something super tasty—cheese! It's like magic: When you churn the milk, it turns into creamy cheese that you can spread on bread or put in your macaroni and cheese.

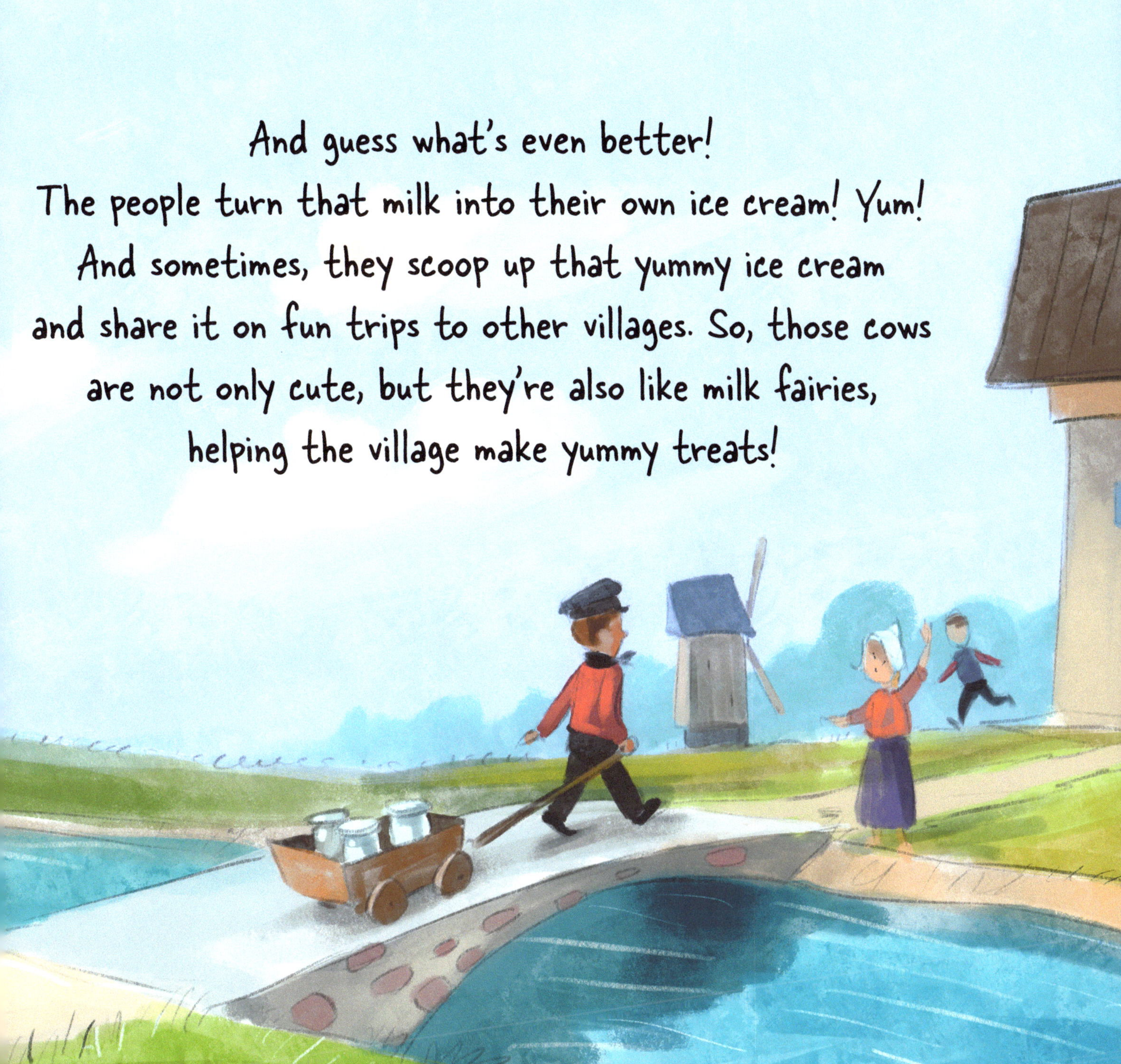

And guess what's even better!
The people turn that milk into their own ice cream! Yum!
And sometimes, they scoop up that yummy ice cream
and share it on fun trips to other villages. So, those cows
are not only cute, but they're also like milk fairies,
helping the village make yummy treats!

Oh, I almost forgot about the shoes. Did you know that people in the Netherlands make their very own wooden shoes! These special shoes are called klompen.

The shoemakers start with blocks of wood, and use their creative magic to shape them into comfy shoes. Imagine walking around in shoes that are made from wood! How awesome is that?

By the way, I love going to the Netherlands in both summer and winter! Do you know why? Because it's like a big adventure playground. In summer, you can hop on a boat and sail down the river, feeling like a captain. Or you can even go for a swim in the water and have a splashing good time! It's a summer wonderland full of watery fun!

In the winter, something magical happens! The river turns into a huge ice skating rink! Can you believe it? I put on my ice skates and glide over the frozen river. Whee! It's like dancing on ice. Winter becomes extra awesome here because I get to have so much fun ice skating!

By the way, Kinderdijk means *children dike*.
Do you know why they gave that name to the village?
Let me explain it to you:

Many years ago, there was a very bad flood in this village. After the flood, the miller saw a baby floating in a cradle on the river. There was also a cat on the cradle, jumping back and forth, trying to keep the cradle balanced so it wouldn't topple over and sink. Since then, people have called this village Kinderdijk.

I hope you enjoyed visiting Kinderdijk with me.

See you on my next adventure...

## Interesting notes to parents

Kinderdijk is a village located in the province of South Holland in the Netherlands.

What makes Kinderdijk truly unique is the concentration and preservation of its windmills. There are 19 windmills in total, all built in the 18th century and situated in close proximity to the waterways. These windmills, with their elegant structures and large rotating blades, create a stunning and quintessentially Dutch landscape. In recognition of their significance, Kinderdijk's windmills were designated as a UNESCO World Heritage Site in 1997, ensuring their protection and cultural legacy for future generations.

The name Kinderdijk translates to "Children's dike" in English, derived from a legendary tale as told by Bozy in the story above.

## About the Author

Mahsan is a medical doctor, working in neuroscience research for most of her career. She is a Persian/American and has lived in the U.S. for 23 years. Following her passion for life and historical places, she has begun writing educational books for children. Mahsan's purpose in writing is to pique children's interest in learning about historical places. This inspiring travel-based series focuses on UNESCO sites and monuments all over the world. Mahsan's goal is for her books to inspire young children, offer interesting information about wonderful places, and show how people lived in the past.

More than a thousand of her Bozy books have already been donated to children's hospitals.